Seven Studies in Pop Piano

Bill Hilton

CARRIER BOOKS

Apapa, Tan yr Onnen, Tregarth, Gwynedd, LL57 4PU

www.billspianopages.com

First published in Great Britain in 2016

A CIP catalogue record for this book
is available from the British Library

ISBN-10 0-9562204-1-X
ISBN-13 978-0-9562204-1-7

Printed by Lightning Source UK Ltd, Milton Keynes

Contents

Introduction

Pop piano – the style you hear from Ben Folds, Elton John, Alicia Keys, Billy Joel, Amanda Palmer, Coldplay's Chris Martin and many others – is very diverse. The pieces in this book are designed to help you learn some of its common features and techniques and give you some practice using them.

In some ways pop piano is a radical style. Some of its distinctive rhythms originate in jazz, rhythm and blues, rock'n'roll and sixties and seventies pop. They often owe more to sounds developed by guitarists and drummers than to previous generations of pianists. Pop pianists often treat the piano as the percussion instrument that it really is, slapping and jabbing on the keyboard to create a raw, crunchy sound. Some of the harmonies the style uses, especially the suspended fourths and ninths we'll come across in the studies, have pushed out the musical boundaries of pop music.

And yet it's also a style deeply rooted in tradition, with clear influences from church, folk and classical music. In some songs you can hear the radical and the traditional side by side. Because of that diversity, it's impossible to do justice to the whole style in a short collection of studies. I've concentrated on what seem to me to be the most common techniques. That has led to some omissions. I should have liked to include a study that covered the recent influence of electronica on pop piano, and a study in waltz time (most pop piano, like most pop music, is in 2/4, 2/2 or 4/4 time, but there several classics in threes, such as Billy Joel's 'Piano Man'). But there we are: perhaps that's material for a later collection.

The majority of pop piano originates in improvisation and is designed to accompany a sung melody. There are some famous pop piano solos and near-solos (Elton John's 'Song for Guy', for example) but they are exceptions to a fairly universal rule. Pop pianists usually start with a melody and a chord progression, and build an improvisation from them. That improvisation may evolve into a settled accompaniment that becomes integral to a song (as in REM's 'Nightswimming'). Or, in true improvisational style, it may vary with each playing.

The aim of this book is to introduce you to some of the approaches and techniques used to create those improvisations. Learning the studies isn't an end in itself. Rather, you should see them as a starting point for your own improvisations.

I'm assuming you have a basic ability at the piano, and that you can at least pick your way through a piano score. If you can, you should find Studies 1 and 2 straightforward enough with practice, and Study 3 only a little more challenging. Studies 4, 5, 6 and 7 are aimed at pianists with intermediate skills – if you've had a few years of formal lessons you shouldn't have many problems. However, if you're a relative beginner you should still be able to pick up useful tips from these more advanced pieces, especially if you look at them alongside the explanatory notes and listen to the accompanying audio files (see 'links', below).

If you've had formal piano lessons you'll have lots of skills that are immensely useful for playing and exploring the studies. Pop piano is probably the genre of popular music that owes the most to the classical tradition. Many of its major figures had a classical education: Billy Joel writes Chopin-esque piano waltzes as well as pop songs; Elton John and Lady Gaga were serious music scholars as children, and Russian-American Regina Spektor is a trained concert pianist. So all those hours you spent practising scales were not in vain – in fact, you should keep practising them!

However, even if you've had that classical education, there will be some things about pop piano you'll find unfamiliar or challenging. For a start, there is scoring complexity. Standard notation evolved to represent the sounds and the rhythms of western classical music. The syncopations of much pop music aren't always easy to write down using the standard system, so pop piano can look harder on the page than it actually is. If at first sight any of the studies look hard, reserve judgment until you've tried playing them – they may be easier than you think. I'll discuss scoring complexity in detail in the notes to Study 3.

I'm also assuming that you know a bit about chords and you've come across popular chord notation (symbols like C, D7, F#m and so on). I'm fully aware that it's possible to have had years of classical lessons and still not know much about pop chords, so in the early studies I've notated the chords in the accompanying notes to give you a helping hand. If you need more help with chords, you might find it useful to watch some of the tutorials on my YouTube channel. You might also find my book *How To Really Play The Piano* useful, as it goes over the groundwork of pop harmony in a fair amount of detail. Links are below.

How to approach the studies

The order you look at the studies and how you learn from them is up to you. What I've tried to do in each case is write a piece of music that illustrates one or more of the skills I think it's useful for you to learn, and then explain those skills, as well as some underlying principles, in the accompanying notes.

If you're a beginner or near beginner, don't assume that you can only learn from the earlier studies. Even if you can't play the later ones up to speed or in their entirety, you'll still find it valuable to go through them and pick up as much as you can. Keep working on your general piano skills, and you'll find you can handle them sooner than you think. As I said, don't be put off by the apparent difficulty of the scores.

If, on the other hand, you're an experienced pianist, don't skip the early studies. Go through them, because they demonstrate ideas that you'll need to understand to make the most of the more advanced studies.

Whatever your level of skill, it's important to remember that pop piano is a fundamentally improvisational style, so in the notes that follow each study I'll be offering some tips on how to improvise on it and generally take it further. If you're new to improvisation it might be useful to pick up some basic skills. Once again, *How To Really Play The Piano* may be helpful here, in particular the chapter that teaches piano improvisation through the medium of twelve-bar blues (which, even if you're not interested in becoming a blues player, is great fun and one of the easiest ways to start improvisation). You'll also find useful material, including a number of beginners' improvisation exercises, among the videos on my YouTube channel.

Some technical stuff

You'll find that the scores in this book are much like any other piano scores. I've used Italian terms to indicate most tempi and techniques, because I think they help universal accessibility, and if you're relatively new to the piano, or have taught yourself to read music, it's good to get to know some of them. All are explained in the notes.

I've marked suggested fingerings throughout the scores, but you should use whatever fingers you feel comfortable with as long as you end up with a well-controlled, musical outcome. I've used standard finger notation (where '1' is the thumb and '5' is the little finger on each hand).

I've also included chord notation above the staff. You should find this helps you to grasp the overall harmonic structure of the each study, and also in some cases to see how I've adapted the underlying chords from the basic progressions. If you decide to improvise on the studies (as I hope you will) then having this notation to give you an ongoing sense of how the progressions work throughout each study should help. Also, if you're classically trained and relatively new to thinking in terms of pop chords, reading them as you go will speed your learning.

There are no phrase markings. This isn't because I don't want you to think about phrasing, but, as I said above, because pop piano is usually played to accompany a singer – so there's not always a melodic line that needs phrasing. That being the case, and given that there's already quite a lot going on above each staff, I decided to leave them out.

I've used the standard British English names for note values. If you're more familiar with the US style, you just need to remember that a semibreve (UK) is a whole note (US); a minim is a half note; a crotchet a quarter note; a quaver an eighth note; and a semiquaver a sixteenth note.

Links

Audio records of each study:
www.billspianopages.com/7-studies/tracks

My YouTube channel:
www.youtube.com/billhiltonbiz

My earlier book, *How To Really Play The Piano*:
www.billspianopages.com/how-to-really

Acknowledgements and thanks

Probably the first people that need thanking are the subscribers to my YouTube channel (70,000 of them at the time of writing and increasing daily), several dozen of whom strongly encouraged me to pursue this project when I floated it as a vague idea in summer 2015.

Thanks to Jeroen van Kleef for ideas and technical advice on notation problems, and to Jeroen (once again) and to Roosmari Croeser for checking the scores and accompanying notes and offering invaluable suggestions. Richard Walshe of www.coincidentalmusic.com was an expert proofreader. Needless to say, any errors that remain are mine alone. Special thanks to Jon Carter, who, during the writing of the book, relentlessly hassled me every time he saw me procrastinating on Facebook.

Special mentions go to those who have supported my Patreon.com crowdfunding campaign over the past few months (see www.patreon.com/billhilton). Supporters who pledge more than $5 per YouTube video I make are promised a special mention in published works. So here they are: Robin Kim, Ray Croc, Alfredo Pegoraro, Ronald Stern, Miyan Levenson, John Moncrieff, Scott Ferguson, Heidi Kuzma, Daniel Gerard, Miss Meowders, Dan Blackwelder, Leslie Nelken, Stephanie Gratzer and Linda Oxley. Thanks very much for your support, guys! I should also particularly single out Amro Gebreel and Matt Kaspar for the high levels of moral support they've offered.

Finally, thanks to Christina for tolerating me while I wrote it, to George – who can now reach the keys by himself – and to Molly the munsterlander, who made me go out on walks. These studies are dedicated to them, with love.

'The piano ain't got no wrong notes.'

Thelonious Monk, March 1976.

Study no. 1

Andante

Study no. 1: chords, dynamics and control

This first study uses some common sounds and techniques from ballad-style and mid-tempo pop piano. The aims of the study are to help you practise good technique and, in the second half of the study, to get your hands working together in a way that's characteristic of pop piano.

There's much more to playing the piano than just pressing the right notes. In fact, sometimes getting the notes totally accurate is less important than good expression and control – topics we'll cover in detail in what follows.

If you're a reasonably experienced pianist, this study and Study 2 might look easy. However, they introduce some of the features of pop piano that you might not be familiar with, so work through them anyway. It's important to get a feel for the quirks of the style!

Harmony

The study is in the key of C major. It uses a simple four bar chord progression based on the chords C, F and G. Here's a summary of the progression:

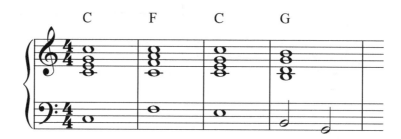

The progression is repeated four times, for a total of sixteen bars. You'll notice that the chords vary a bit throughout the study. Sometimes they have bass notes other than the note they are named after. So, for example, in the first bar of the study the chord is C, with C (the note) in the bass. But in the third bar the chord is C with E in the bass.

I could notate this as 'C/E' ('C over E' or 'C with an E in the bass'). In the summary above I've shown two common alternative bass notes – E under a C chord ('C/E') and B under a G chord ('G/B'). In later studies I'll use that form of notation. In this one, however, I've just given the basic chord name in the interest of keeping things clear. As you work through the studies, listen out for the effects different bass notes have on chords. A different bass note changes what we call the 'voicing' of the chord.

In the second half of the study I've enriched some of the chords. In bars 10 and 14 the basic chord of F becomes F(add9) and in bars 12 and 15 the basic chords of G and G7 becomes G(sus4) and G7(sus4). You'll sometimes see chords like this written as 'Gsus' or 'G7sus', without the '4'. We'll think more about added ninths and sus ("suspended") chords in Study 4.

For now, just listen to the sound these chords make, and notice how easy it is to create them: you move your fingers less than you do to make the basic forms of the chords.

Fingering

Pop pianists don't need to be quite as obsessive as classical pianists about fingering, but it's still useful to think about how best to get your fingers from note to note smoothly and logically. In this study the right-hand fingering is simple, because that hand barely changes position on the piano keyboard.

In the left, though, I've made things a bit more interesting, with some fingers-over and thumbs-under. It might seem unnecessarily complicated, but follow the fingering carefully and you'll see how it makes the bassline smoother and – here's that word again – more even. You might find it helps to play the left hand by itself a few times.

Expression

The way you play the notes is as important as the notes themselves: it's pointless getting them right if you're just bashing away without a sense of musicality. You need to produce something musically satisfying, and that means working on what musicians call *expression*. Expression is a broad subject that covers a lot of different techniques, but good expression always involves thinking about:

- **Evenness and control.** Playing evenly doesn't mean playing each note exactly the same, but rather exercising control so that the notes sound rounded and musical, and get louder and softer when you want them to. In this study, for example, the broken chords (see below) should sound even: you want to avoid an irregular *CLUNK-clunk-CLUNK-clunk* kind of sound.

- **Dynamics.** The study starts soft (*p*) and at various points is moderately loud (*mf*), loud (*f*) and very soft (*pp*). Notice the 'hairpins' for *crescendo* (getting louder...) and *decrescendo* (getting softer...). Keep an eye on them, and make a point of getting louder and softer gradually and evenly. At first this might seem trivial, but it's as important as playing the notes right in the first place.

Because of its importance in pop piano and the ways it's used, we might also add:

- **Pedal.** In this kind of playing it's a good idea to use a bit of sustain (right) pedal to smooth out the chords and give the overall sound more depth and presence. Feel free to play around with the pedal in this study, but I've not marked any pedalling in the way I have in later studies. Watch out, though: the sustain pedal is also pretty good at hiding bad technique – or, at least, burying it in a mush of sound. You'll get the most out of this study if you practise it without pedal at first, and focus on good expression and control.

Study 1: bar-by-bar breakdown

Bars 1-8

First, let's think about tempo. *Andante* is slow, but not too slow. It means 'at a walking pace'. So you're walking rather than running – but you shouldn't be dawdling either. Make sure you stick fairly strictly to time. Try not to rush through the easy bars then slow down for the trickier ones. Keep everything the same speed all the way through.

In the right hand we've got a type of broken chord pattern that's common in pop piano. I call these 'split chords', because you make them by taking a simple chord (C major in the first bar), splitting it into two parts (notes C and E+G) and alternating them in a rocking pattern.

If you find it difficult to stick to a regular tempo playing split chords, try using a metronome (or a metronome app, of which there are many available) to beat the rhythm for you. *Andante* starts around 80 beats per minute (bpm). Metronomes are useful, but sometimes they are quite difficult to play along with. Trying to stick to the very precise metronome beat for a whole piece can cause you to lose focus on other important things, like expression. Use the metronome in short sections where it's important you get the timing right.

Back to the study. Things start fairly quietly, but then the volume begins to swell gradually in bar three before dropping down again at bar 5. Make sure you handle the *crescendo* smoothly: you should get gradually louder over the course of bars 3-4 and 7-8 rather than increasing the volume all at once.

Bars 9-12

Two things change here. Firstly, the chords are altered very slightly – but that shouldn't give you too much trouble, as your hand position doesn't change.

There's also a new rhythm in the left. This is a useful and common left hand pattern, as it mimics one of the most basic (and, in fact, somewhat clichéd) bass guitar licks. If you find it tricky at first, take it slowly, and mentally cue up left and right hand notes with each other: the second note of each bar in the left (a quaver) is played exactly at the same time as the third quaver in the right, and so on.

One thing to watch out for is that playing the new rhythm in the left hand doesn't mess up the evenness of your right: it's easy to come down harder on those right hand notes that are played at the same time as a left hand note. Keep it steady and even: your hands are working together, certainly, but they're still doing different things.

The *rit.* in bar 12 means 'slow down here'. It can be short for *ritenuto* or *ritardando*. Classical musicians find shades of difference between the two, but among composers they are used in varying ways, and sometimes interchangeably. Gradually ease the tempo, building tension for a couple of beats. Return to the original speed at the *a tempo* marking in bar 13.

Bars 13-16

Quite a bit of new stuff starts to happen as we approach the end of the study. Note the left hand going into octaves in the last two bars. At the same time everything gets softer until the final notes are played *pp* – very soft. It takes a bit of practice to get the notes that quiet, and keep them even, while playing octaves in the left. Keep going until you have a steady *decrescendo* in bar 13, and make sure the left hand isn't too clunky and dominant.

Taking it further

There's lots of scope for improvisation in this study. The best way to start is probably just to play around with the rhythm. As you can see from the second half of the study (bar 9 onwards) one of the ways pop piano creates a sense of rhythm and drive is by creating cross-rhythms between the two hands.

If you've ever done any drumming, this should come naturally – building rhythmic tension between the hands is what a drummer does between hi-hat and snare, especially when playing more complex break-beats. In fact, a great deal of pop piano, and especially up-tempo material, involves using the piano as a percussion instrument as much as a melodic and harmonic one. That sometimes affects the way we physically play the keys, as we'll see in Study 4.

For now, see if you can create more complex rhythms of your own, just using the chord shapes in the study, either splitting the chords or leaving them unsplit, depending on what feels right. If that seems a bit daunting, start by improvising on just the first bar – the chord of C, in effect – over and over. As with all improvisation, the secret is to suspend judgment on yourself – it doesn't matter if it sounds terrible at first.

You might also like to play around with some of those more complex sus4 and add9 chords. I'll discuss these in more detail in the notes to Study 4, but for now try experimenting with them in this progression. Where else can you take them?

Study no. 2

Study no. 2: minor key broken chords and arpeggios

The aim of this study is to work on some more types of broken chord and get you thinking about the way you organise your fingers to play smoothly and efficiently.

First, some terminology. *Broken chord* is the catch-all term for a sequence of notes, played in any combination or order, that all come from a single underlying chord. An *arpeggio* is similar but different: it is the individual notes of a chord played one at a time, in order, up or down (or up and then down, or down and up). An arpeggio can rise and/or fall by as few as three notes, or it can travel the length of the piano keyboard.

When you have some experience as a pianist, arpeggio patterns are very natural, obvious things to play on a keyboard, and are common in classical piano. As I said in the Introduction, many famous pop pianists have a classical training. So it's not surprising that bits and pieces of the classics, such as arpeggios, have seeped into the style.

There are some easy parts and some slightly harder parts to this study. You should aim to play the whole thing confidently, and at a consistent tempo.

Harmony

Once again we have a four-chord loop, only this time in a minor key:

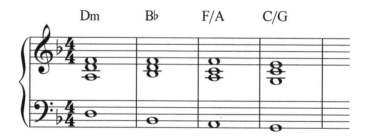

The loop is repeated six times, with some slight changes towards the end of the study. In the last eight bars the right hand chords start to be set against left hand arpeggios that begin on the root note of the chord in each case. So, for example, bars 19 and 20 revert to using a root position F chord and a root position C chord (an F in the bass and a C in the bass at the start of each left-hand arpeggio) rather than the voicings in the outline progression above.

Fingering

When you're playing in an arpeggiated style, choosing and using good fingering makes all the difference. Well-fingered, your playing will sound smoother and more natural, and you'll be able to be much more expressive. Ballad-style pop piano isn't quite as demanding as classical piano, and you can use the sustain pedal to cover quite a bit of jumping around. However, using your fingers well makes it much easier to produce a flowing, confident sound.

I've included suggested fingering, but any reasonably sensible fingering you pick for this study should help you practise moving fingers and thumb over each other in both hands. It will also work your fourth and fifth fingers, which pianists new to improvisatory styles sometimes neglect in favour of the stronger thumb, second and third fingers. When playing arpeggios, try to keep your hands and fingers relaxed. If you tense up the result is more likely to be uneven, and you might even strain yourself on the bigger stretches.

Expression
This study gives you a few interesting little challenges when it comes to expression:

- **Evenness and control.** As in the previous two studies, evenness really matters here. In particular, make sure that you're not thumping the first note of every bar, or the first note of every group of four quavers. If you have good control you can give the study a great deal of expression just with the dynamic ebb and flow within each broken chord group.

- **Dynamics.** I've marked the first bar *p* (soft) and the feeling of restraint that implies should dominate the study. Things do get louder at a couple of points, but there are no really dramatic changes from soft to loud. Make sure each *crescendo* is gradual and steady. This should give the study quite a dark, intense feel.

- **Pedal.** You need to use the sustain pedal in this study. By the way, any *ped* or *con pedale* marking always means use the sustain (right) pedal. If the composer wants you to use the soft (left) pedal, he or she will mark the score *una corda*. You can still use the soft pedal in this study if you want to, but it's the sustain pedal that's important.

  The type of pedal line I've used under the stave implies lifting the pedal just enough to cut off the sustain effect, then pushing down again straight away. On most pianos this only needs a slight movement of the ankle to achieve. You shouldn't take your foot fully off the pedal before you put it back down again.

Study 2: bar-by-bar breakdown

Bars 1-4
The study starts very simply, with three bars of block chords, and a fourth bar that forms a lead-in to the broken chords that start in bar 5. The dynamic marking is *p* (soft), so you should do your best to make sure that each one sounds soft, rich and even. The changes between them should be smooth, and each note in each chord should be played at exactly the same volume.

The wiggly lines to the left of the first few chords in the right hand are arpeggiation marks. You should 'spread' these chords, pressing and holding each note in turn, from bottom to top, until the full chord is sounding. This kind of arpeggiation is always quick, or quick-ish: it should be noticeable that the notes are coming down individually, but that's all – just lay down the chord, and don't linger over the individual notes.

Bars 5-8

In these few bars we move on to a simple broken chord pattern in the right hand. Again, you're aiming for evenness, but that doesn't mean each note needs to be exactly identical. What you should aim to do is to give each bar, or even each half bar, a sense of *shape*: you could, for example, 'swell' each group of four quavers so that the highest note in each group is a noticeable high point in terms of intensity. The trick is to make this effect subtle, and perhaps to vary it between bars for an expressive effect. Above all, remember to listen to the sound you're making. Does it sound smooth and musical? Watch out for the pairs of notes on the first half beats of bars 6, 7 and 8. You're on and off these pretty quickly, but you need to keep them even and ensure they don't create too noticeable a 'thump' at the start of their bars.

Don't forget to get slightly louder with the *crescendo* hairpin in bar eight, and note the change in the left hand rhythm.

Bars 9-12

Not much changes in the right hand here except for the shape of the broken chords. There's a slightly wider stretch – which offers new expressive possibilities, especially on the higher notes – but you should continue in pretty much the same vein as before, albeit with a slightly louder, fuller sound. The new left-hand rhythm has established itself, but it's still quite simple: we're just adding movement in preparation for some more complex cross-rhythms later in the study. Again, take note of the *crescendo* at the end of this subsection, in bar 12.

Bars 13-16

This is where things begin to look a little trickier in the right hand. Actually, though, the pattern of block chords that comes in here isn't too hard. As long as you can play the chords evenly and comfortably, it should sound fine. You'll find that there's a natural stress on those half beats that contain a chord. That's an important part of the developing rhythm, but shouldn't be too obvious. Look closely, too, at the left hand rhythm that appears in bar 16: it's going to come up again in the right hand at the start of the next bar. On the face of it, it might seem an awkward rhythm to play: dotted crotchet, dotted crotchet, crotchet. Actually, it's fairly easy, and mimics the right hand stress pattern we've just seen marked out by the chords in the right. If you're not sure about it at first, try counting eight quavers to the bar rather than four crotchets (you can do that just by adding 'and' to the crotchet count: '1-and 2-and 3-and 4-and...'). Think of each dotted crotchet as three quavers and the final crotchet as two, for a total of eight in the bar. This is a really important rhythm to get the hang of, and it will crop up again in later studies, so it's worth taking the time to get it right.

You might also notice that something interesting is happening to the chords in bars 13 and 14. Instead of Dm and Bb, the chords in these bars have become more complex: Dm7 and Bb(add9). We'll discuss this process of adding complexity to pop piano chords in Study 4.

Bars 17-20

Your hands are moving quite a lot now, and the dynamic is *f* (loud) – we're at the climactic moment of the study. Don't lose control here, especially on those arpeggio patterns in the left, and remember that although it's supposed to be 'loud' that doesn't mean 'deafening' or 'out of control'. Let the piano sing out by all means, but there should be a definite sense of control. The right hand is playing the dotted crotchet, dotted crotchet, crotchet pattern we discussed above. If you're struggling with it here, measure it out against the quavers in the left. You might find it worthwhile to practise this section hands separately at first.

Some of the fingering in the left is tricky, by the way – especially on the Bb chord in bar 18. If you struggle to put your fingers over each other and play this really *legato*, don't be afraid to jump – it'll be a little less elegant, but the pedal will help to hold things together.

Bars 21-25

Everything goes suddenly (*subito*) soft, and we're back to the simple broken chord pattern in the right hand. In the left, though, we now have the dotted crotchet, dotted crotchet, crotchet pattern, which should give the whole thing a clear sense of forward rhythm and energy, even though the volume is low. The final chord, like the first, is arpeggiated.

Taking it further

Arpeggios (and broken chords in general) really lend themselves to improvisation. One way you could take this exercise further is by having a go at improvising a greater range of arpeggios and broken chords on this chord progression, in both left and right hands.

You can also use the other progressions in the book – and, in fact any chord progression – as the basis for improvising on broken chords and arpeggios. They're one of the most useful tools in the pop pianist's toolbox, so it's worth spending some time getting comfortable with them.

Study no. 3

Quite slowly

con ped.

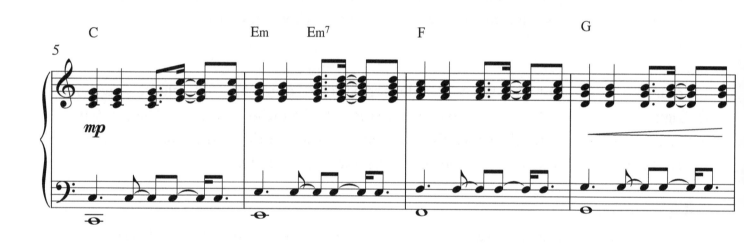

Study no. 3: working across the beat

As I said in the Introduction, one of the challenges you have to face when you start playing pop piano is the way that its rhythms can differ both from conventional classical rhythms you may have learned from piano lessons, and also from the more swinging rhythms of jazz and blues.

Pop piano's characteristic rhythms aren't hard to play – in fact, once you have a feel for the style you should find them very natural. But because they often work across beats rather than squarely on them, they can be hard to write down in standard notation. This study will show you how a typical pop piano rhythm works, and help you see past the apparent complexity of the notation to the straightforward music underneath.

Harmony

After the simple loops of the first two studies, Study 3 uses a more complex chord progression. You can split it into two halves. The first half starts in the major, with a C chord, and goes on a journey to the dominant chord, G, in bar 8:

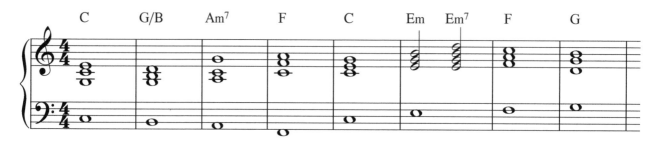

That G sets up the expectation of a return to the tonic chord, C. However, the progression defies that expectation by starting the second half of the study in the minor, with a Dm chord in bar 9. The journey from there is back to the tonic, C, in bar 16:

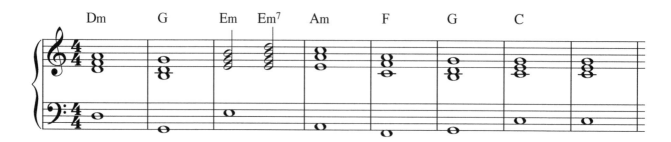

There are a couple of interesting notation quirks that are worth mentioning. First, the Am7 chord in bar 3 is missing its E, as I prefer the clearer, barer sound of the A-C-G combination at that point in the piece. However, I've still notated it as Am7, as that remains the underlying chord, and I'd want anyone using the chords for accompaniment (perhaps on an instrument like the guitar) or improvisation to understand that.

Second, there are various chords that I could notate in greater detail, but don't. So, strictly speaking the chord on the first beat of bar 4 is F(add9) rather than just plain F, and the chord on the first quarter beat of bar 12 is Am(sus4) rather than just Am. In each case I've decided that labelling those suspensions as different chords isn't worth the extra complexity. Chord symbols aren't supposed to describe a piece of music in every last detail, but to give a structural overview of its harmony. I'll discuss this more in the notes to Study 4.

Rhythm

The rhythms may look complicated at first, but they're straightforward to play. As I said in the Introduction, we're running into the problem of using classical notation for some decidedly un-classical rhythms. The thing to remember is that each hand's rhythm often runs across the other's, and each can also work across the beat. The tension that results from that beat-crossing creates the pulse and sense of forward movement you hear in a lot of pop piano.

If you find it difficult to work out the rhythm, you need to identify exactly where each of the four beats lies in the bar. Here's how you might do that with bar 1:

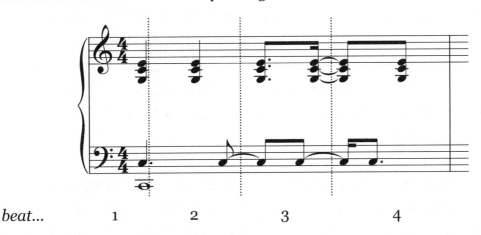

Work out the rhythm of each beat, subdividing into half-beats or quarter-beats if necessary, perhaps hands separately at first. The stick the whole thing together. You'll see that I've used note groupings and ties to make the position of each beat fairly clear. Sometimes when you're notating there's a conflict between keeping the score tidy and maintaining the sense of where the beat is. In later studies you'll notice that I sometimes compromise for the sake of tidiness, and have (for example) a crotchet crossing the second half of one beat and the first half of the next. Even when things are scored in that slightly more compressed way, you should still be able to split the bar down into beats to make sense of the rhythm.

If that's proving difficult (or you just want confirmation that you've got it right!) listen to me play it in the audio files that accompany the book – see the Introduction for details.

Fingering

You don't have to worry too much about the fingering in this study, as none of it is hard, and to a certain extent you can use the pedal to stick things together (see below). However, it's still useful to make fingering choices that minimize the amount of jumping you have to do. With that in mind I've made some fingering suggestions in a few places.

My suggested fingering is quite jumpy compared to the sort of fingering a classical pianist might use. But part of the point of pop piano – and a factor that contributes to its distinctive sound – is that it should be relaxed and unfussy. Making a jump and covering it with the pedal is OK in in a way that might not be if you were playing, say, Bach.

Expression

Even though it's using fairly chunky block chords in the right, this is a gentle and expressive piece. When you're playing it, listen carefully to yourself and focus on making the sound as rich and expressive as possible

- **Evenness and control.** You'll find that this study is quite unforgiving of uneven playing. You need to take particular care over the chords in the right hand, and make sure that you give each chord's notes equal weight. That can be tricky when you're getting louder or softer, so you might find it useful to practise the right hand on its own at first. As with any piano piece you should try to avoid seeing it as a purely mechanical exercise, a test that you've 'passed' if you get to the end having played all the right notes. Always listen to what you're playing – that's when you'll spot unevenness, and the poor expression that results from it.

- **Dynamics.** Notice that the whole thing is relatively soft, with extremes ranging from *mf* (moderately loud) to *pp* (very soft). The softness is deliberate: playing repeated block chords at low volume is more challenging than bashing them out loudly. Try to make sure that the *mf* section is a noticeable peak in the study, but still not too loud.

- **Pedal.** I've marked the score *con ped.* (*con pedale*, with pedal) which means you should use the sustain pedal at your discretion. Unlike Study 2, I haven't marked any specific pedalling, but left you to work it out for yourself. You'll probably find pedalling with every chord change works well, but you can vary things, too, pedalling lightly or more heavily depending on the expressive effect you're after. You can also use the sustain pedal to cover some of the larger right-hand jumps if you wish.

Study 3: bar-by-bar breakdown

Bars 1-8

Everything starts quite softly here, before growing in volume a little during bar 4. As we said above, evenness is important: in particular, make sure that the hint of melody created by the upper notes of the chords is clear. So, when you jump from the G chord in root position in the first two beats of bar 2 up to the first inversion of the chord, starting on the third beat, make sure your fifth finger is coming down on the G at the top of the latter chord just as firmly as all your other fingers are. If you're not careful, some fingers can come down more strongly or weakly than others within chords, leading to unevenness. This is a particular risk if you're playing quite softly, as is the case here.

In terms of evenness and control, also watch out for the start of bar 4, where the F chord on the first beat has a suspended G. The resolution on to the A on the second beat should be clear and smooth.

Bars 9-16

There's a build-up in intensity here: the Dm chords in bar 9 should be the loudest in the study so far – but don't make them too loud. If we think about the overall dynamic shape of the piece then bars 9 to 11 represent a peak, the most important part of the journey. From bar 12 on things get softer again, and the study begins to travel towards 'home', to its end.

It's always useful to think about the overall shape of a piece of music, however short it is, and also about its dynamic and emotional structure. Doing that helps you move beyond simply 'getting through it' and helps you create a convincing, authentic musical performance.

A really critical part of the study is the transition from bar 11 to bar 12. The Em chords in 11 are rich and intense. The suspended D in the Am chord at the start of 12 is a falling-off from this intensity and marks the beginning of the *diminuendo* back down to the stability of the *mp* (moderately soft) F chord in bar 13. There's a lot of scope for expressivity there: play around with it and see what you can achieve. Remember to listen intently to the sound you're making every time you play it.

Note the rhythmic variations in the right hand in bars 12 and 13. There's also variation in the left in bars 13 and 14. Make sure the rising notes in the left hand in bars 13 and 14 are even and natural, and contribute to the whole sound rather than dominating it – you'll find they easily become clunky if you don't pay careful attention to what you're doing.

Taking it further

You can use the rhythmic pattern in this study with more or less any chord progression. Try lifting a progression from elsewhere (perhaps one of the other studies, or a favourite song) and using the pattern with it.

Alternatively, see how you can vary the pattern. What happens if you try to simplify it, make it more complex, or take it at a different tempo? A faster tempo, especially, might force you to reconsider the way you use the pedal and even the way you physically play the notes. Would a more aggressive, percussive approach – such as we're about to look at in Study 4 – work better at those higher speeds?

Study no. 4

Study no. 4: jumping around

This study, although it's challenging in a few places, gives you scope to let rip! It's designed to improve your ability to make fairly quick jumps, to play unison octaves precisely (a useful skill, and not as simple as it looks) and to help you build your hand independence in cross rhythms. It's not fundamentally hard to play, but it might take you a while to get everything absolutely fluent and precise.

Harmony

It's worth thinking about the harmony of this study in detail. It may seem academic, but there's some interesting harmonic stuff going on here, including the creation of harmonies that are very common in pop piano. When I started to write the study I had a simple four-bar chord loop in mind, similar to the ones we saw in Studies 1 and 2:

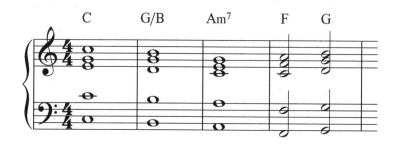

However, as you can see if you look back at the first four bars of the study, the actual chords that I ended up with are rather different:

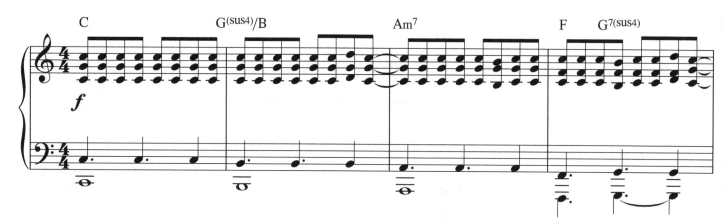

That's because they have been through a process of *extension* and *substitution*. The whole thing is still, in fact, based on that four-bar loop, and if you were playing along with a rhythm section you could quite easily give the guitarist and bassist the basic form of the chords to play – it would all sound fine. You can think of the new chords as an enrichment of the basic ones: still the same chords, but changed to create a more interesting sound.

It's worth noting is how I've reached those apparently exotic chords like suspended fourths ('sus4') and added ninths ('add9'). In most cases it's not by moving my right hand more, to adopt a more complex position – it's by moving it *less*. So, in bar 2, rather than changing to a position that might suit the underlying G chord, I continue the partial C chord pattern from bar 1. This creates a chord that we could label in various ways, but which I've called G(sus4)/B (the full chord would also require a D). We'll look at some of the individual chords in detail in the bar-by-bar breakdown, over the page.

That process happens repeatedly during the study. You can see another variant of it in bars 21-28, where I use resolving suspensions for a different harmonic effect – we'll discuss that in more detail below.

There are also several places where the chords are ambiguous and/or incomplete. In other words, you could label them in more than one way, or they are so incomplete that it doesn't make sense to label them at all (hence the 'no chord' markings in bars 13-20 and 33-35). The very first chord, for example, is labelled C major, but as played in the study it only contains the notes C and G. C major should also have an E. That note is missing, so the chord doesn't have its full identity: it could, in principle, be C minor or some other chord containing the notes C and G. We can label it C major because of its context. Playing the piece as a whole, it's fairly obvious that it is in the key of C major and that the first chord is C, with or without its E. The reason I've missed out the E, by the way, has much to do with the way the piece is played – again, I'll discuss that in more detail below.

I'm talking about this situation at some length because piano learners often like very definite answers about chords and the way they are described – but once things start to get beyond the basics, definite answers can be hard to find. The Wikipedia entry for pop chord notation (i.e., the letter symbols we're dealing with here, such a G, Em and so on) says '... *this notation does not easily provide for ways of describing all chords*'. That's a bit of an understatement.

It's worth remembering that the chord notation used for jazz and pop music is a shorthand that's evolved over the years to help performing musicians do their job. It wasn't developed by academics trying to create a rigorous system, but by working musicians who needed a quick and readable way of writing down chords. In consequence, while there are conventions governing the way individual chords are notated, there's a certain amount of flexibility, and the overall aim is simply that the notation should offer a convenient overview of the harmony (since jazz and pop musicians tend to improvise a lot, absolute precision about, say, a chord's voicing or exact inversion isn't usually necessary). That means we can sometimes run into problems when we try to use pop chord notation to represent complex harmonies or particular voicings.

So where does that leave us? The best advice when you're unsure what a chord is or whether it's 'right' is to ask yourself: does it sound good? If you're playing with other people, or accompanying yourself or someone else singing, you should also ask: does it seem to fit the original, underlying chord progression? If the answer to both questions is 'yes', you don't need to worry too much about what the chord is called, or whether it 'should' be where it is.

A note on anticipation

There are many instances of rhythmic anticipation here, especially in the right hand – in other words, places where the chord comes in half a beat before it's 'supposed' to, and is tied across the bar line. Here's an example between bars 6 and 7:

When there's an anticipation like this, I've notated the chord as changing at the start of the new bar, even though the change (at least in the right hand) is actually happening half a beat earlier. This keeps the harmonic structure clear and easy to read, which you'll find useful if you create your own improvisations based on the progression. I've followed the same practice in Studies 5, 6 and 7.

Fingering

I haven't marked any fingering in this study, but you'll still need to give some thought to the best fingers to use for individual chord shapes.

In the context of this kind of playing, the choices you make will be governed much more by what you personally find comfortable than by the need to play in a flowing, *legato* style.

Expression

As we saw in Study 2, one of the common features of the pop style is that it often treats the piano as a percussion instrument as well as a melodic and harmonic one. The percussive effect many pop pianists use in up-tempo pieces is mostly just a case of moving your hands more and using a relatively loose, bouncing lower arm – a somewhat similar action to the one you might use if you were playing a set of bongos with the flats of your hands. Take care not to let your wrists get too floppy, though, as it's important to retain control of what you're playing.

I mentioned on the previous page that I've written those wide right-hand chords with three notes rather than four for a reason. It's because a widely-spread hand with just three fingers in use makes that percussive attack easier (try dropping an E into the first C chord and see how much trickier it is to play in a percussive style). As I said on the previous page, this has the effect of robbing the chord of a note, but makes this kind of expression much easier. 'Thinning out' the chord also adds a certain amount of clarity to the sound, and reduces the sort of muddiness that might result from many closely-spaced notes being played loudly, especially on acoustic pianos or in situations where there is lots of echo or reverb.

- **Evenness and control.** There are two main challenges here. The first is to keep to time during jumps. Don't speed up for the easy bits only to slow down when you have to move your hand. Better to practise the whole thing at a slow tempo before speeding up.

    The second is to keep your playing under control and make sure there's a contrast between louds and softs. You can put a lot of energy into the louds, but it should never sound as if you're just beating the piano. There should always be a sense of control.

- **Dynamics.** These are pretty straightforward. The one challenging bit is keeping the overall sound soft and even (*p*) during those big octave leaps in bars 13-20. You should be able to do this pretty easily with practice: the overall effect should be that you're placing your fifth finger and thumb on each octave in a deliberate, measured way, rather than desperately leaping from octave to octave. If necessary, practise the right hand by itself until you get the dynamic just right.

- **Pedal.** You can pedal pretty much at your discretion in this study. You should find that you don't need too much, but pedal will be useful in giving a richer sound and sticking some of the jumps together. Experiment with using lots of pedal and then a bit less, and notice the difference.

Bar-by-bar breakdown

Bars 1-12
The study is at a medium tempo. The metronome mark at the top of the score suggests 100 beats per minute, but you don't need to play the study at exactly that speed (the same goes for the metronome marks in all the later studies). I've added a bit of interest by including some tied notes across bars, which makes the rhythm a little more complex. If you struggle to get the left hand going right away, use the technique I suggested in Study 3, and count the dotted crotchets and crotchet against the quavers in the right. Note the effect in bar 4, where the lower notes of a G octave are tied (you'd probably use your fifth finger) while the upper are not tied, but played a separate notes, probably with your thumb.

The two slightly unusual chords we come across here are G(sus4) and F(add9), which you might also see written without the parentheses and, in the case of the sus chord, possibly without the number 4 (i.e., 'Gsus'). However, if you're unsure about these two, or need a reminder, G(sus4) is a regular G chord with an added ('suspended') C, the fourth note above the root, G. The third (B in the chord of G) is often missed out or played elsewhere to avoid a very obvious discord with the neighbouring C. Here, I've gone a step further and taken out the D, too, so the right hand 'chord' just consists of Gs and Cs, while the B reappears in the bass.

F(add9) is a regular F chord with a ninth added, usually immediately next to the F itself. The ninth is the same as the second, so F(add9) is an F chord with a G added. As with sus chords, the third (A in an F chord) is often missed out.

Bars 13-20

The octave jumps here aren't as hard as they look, though they may take some practice. The challenge is to keep the right hand accurate and precise, but also relatively quiet (I've marked this section *p*). Note the slight variation in the left hand in bar 20. It continues in the equivalent bars of the chord loop for the rest of this study.

Bars 21-28

In this section we meet a whole succession of suspended ninth sounds – in this case, the D suspended then resolving up to an E in the overall framework of a C chord in a repeated lick (travelling downwards in bars 21-24 and upwards in 25-28). There's a tricky bit of fingering to deal with here: the D-E resolution that crosses beats 2 and 3 of each bar, as here, in bar 24:

Pretty much the only way of playing this, unless you have very large and flexible hands, is to play both notes with your thumb, which means jumping. You'll probably be using the pedal at this point to stick things together, and that should cover any potential lumpiness. You still have to be pretty quick with your thumb, though!

Bars 29-37

There's nothing really new in the final eight bars. The main challenge is to make the *diminuendo* in bars 33-36 even and steady – don't get too quiet too quickly, but gradually reduce the volume until the final notes in bar 37 are as soft as possible. There's a rit. (see p.12) in bar 36, which should make it easier to make that final suspended ninth resolution really soft.

Taking it further

The main things to take out of this study are the percussive style of playing and the ways in which the chords are easily changed by limiting hand movement. You could try improvising on the study using different chord inversions in the right hand, and seeing what kind of chords and sounds develop from the process.

Study no. 5

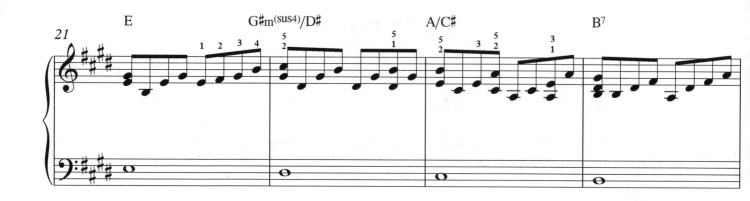

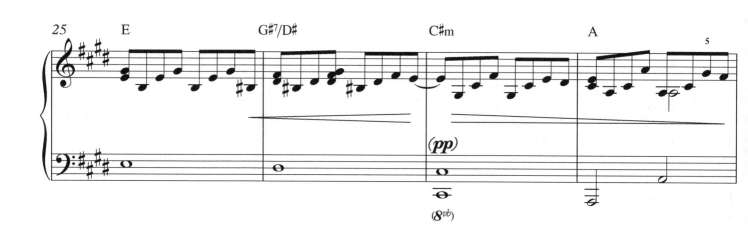

Study no. 5: a ballad

This is a ballad-type study that starts in a fairly free, relaxed style. However, as it develops it needs a strong forward drive, or you'll find that the right hand broken chords that appear from bar 17 onwards will get bogged down. The challenge is to be expressive while keeping a clear sense of direction and control.

Even though this isn't a blazingly quick piece – you could take the first dozen or so bars really quite slowly – I've scored it in 2/2 time. In practical terms this isn't very different from 4/4 at this kind of tempo, but you might find that counting two beats to the bar rather than four helps to give it a better flow.

All the studies so far have been in fairly easy keys. This one is in E major, with four sharps. That makes it a bit harder, but it's useful and important to get used to playing in a variety of keys. There are three basic reasons for that:

• Many songs are in keys that are quite difficult for pianists. E and A, in particular, are popular keys because they are relative easy for guitarists. It's important to get comfortable in those keys if you want to play other people's songs (without transposing) or play in a band.

• Different keys fall under your fingers differently, and therefore encourage different approaches to improvisation. Being able to play and improvise in a diversity of keys will widen the skills and sounds available to you. That's useful if you want to write and record your own songs – your first album won't sound very impressive if all the tracks are in the same key!

• An important musicianship skill, especially for improvisers, is adaptability. You'll find that by playing in a variety of keys you improve your ability to play in all of them.

Harmony

The chord progression in this study is, at sixteen bars, the longest we've seen so far. It's repeated three times, and varies slightly each time. To create it, I started with a very basic looped progression, which in its simplest form looks like this:

E | B | C#m | A |
E | Emaj7 | A | B, A |
E | G#7 | C#m | A |
E | E | A | B ...

From there, I added a descending bass pattern, which put some of the chords into different voicings – that is to say, gave some of the chords bass notes different from their root notes, a common effect we first came across in Study 1:

(bars 1-4)	E | B/D# | C#m | A |
(bars 5-8)	E | Emaj7/D# | A | B, A |
(bars 9-12)	E | G#7/D# | C#m | A
(bars 13-16)	E | E/G# | A | B ...

When it came to working that progression up into an actual piece of music, I varied it quite a bit and used several extended and subsituted chords. In the final version, for example, the Emaj7 chord in bar 6 has vanished altogether (becoming B(sus4)/D in the first and third runs through of the progression, and G#m(sus4)/D# in the second, which sounds complex but isn't if you look at it). And in the third run through I've replaced bars 5-8 of the progression with a repeat of bars 1-4 (bars 37-40 of the study).

An important effect in the progression is the so-called plagal cadence. If you don't know the term, a 'cadence' is a sequence of chords – usually two – that ends a phrase or section within a piece of music. Very often this will involve a return to the tonic chord. The most well-known and obvious cadence is V—>I (the chord built on the fifth note of the scale of the key resolving to the chord built on the first note; that is from the dominant chord to the tonic chord, e.g. G—>C in the key of C major, B—>E in the key of E major). It's sometimes known as a perfect cadence.

The plagal cadence is IV—>I: that is, F—>C in the key of C major, and A—>E in the key of E major. It's sometimes called the 'amen cadence' because it is often used to sing that word at the ends of hymns (sometimes in decorated form: see below).

The study's progression can be broken down into four 4-bar section bars: the first, second and third end on the chord of A (chord IV) leading to E (chord I) at the start of the following section (plagal cadences) while the final one ends on the stronger dominant chord, B (chord V) to create a perfect cadence.*

Fingering
None of the fingering in this study is really difficult, and as in the previous studies I've marked in my suggestions.

Expression
When it comes to dynamics and evenness and control, there's not much going on in this study that we haven't already seen in previous studies – but it's a good opportunity to put

*Strictly speaking these are half cadences, because each phrase ends without resolving to the tonic. Also, in the final version of the study the | B,A | in bar eight of the progression has been replaced with a full bar of B.

some lessons we've already learned into practice. I'll mention specific evenness and control issues as they arise, in the bar-by-bar breakdown. However, there are two things we do need to think about:

- **Rubato.** The expression marking at the start of the study is *tempo rubato*. In Italian this literally means 'robbed time', and traditionally means playing in a rhythmically flexible way without slackening the overall tempo of the music, by 'robbing' time from some beats and giving it to others. For most of the twentieth century, though, the term has been use in a more general sense to indicate that a piece can be played with rhythmic freedom and without a strict metre. So rather than sticking to a rigid 'one-two-three-four' at *x* beats per minute, you can speed up or slow down as you feel necessary to make the music more expressive.

  Revert to playing to a tighter pulse at the *tempo giusto* ('strict time') marking in bar 17. Even then, though, it's up to you: you might find that a little bit of added *rubato* can add interest throughout, especially towards the end of the piece.

  It's worth noting that *rubato* is easiest when playing as a solo pianist or singing and playing simultaneously. If you're playing in a band, the rhythm section will generally not play during *rubato* sections. If you're accompanying a singer (rather than singing yourself) and intend to use *rubato*, you either need to have practised a great deal in advance, and/or have eye contact, and/or have practised so carefully that you can anticipate the *rubato* independently of one another.

- **Pedal.** Rather than marking in the pedalling here I've just added the direction *con ped.* at the start. So how and where you use the sustain pedal is up to you, and will depend on your particular interpretation of the study.

Study 5: bar-by-bar breakdown

Bars 1-16

The study begins with some fairly straightforward right hand patterns over a simple left hand, at a moderate tempo, although the *rubato* marking gives us leeway to vary the speed bar-by-bar. As we've seen in previous studies, the rhythm is working across the beat here, particularly in bars 2-4. None of it is too hard, but it might be worth practising the first four bars in the right hand until you've got a feel for the rhythm.

In bar 4 we come across one of the characteristic sounds of pop piano: a root position chord with a suspended second (which, when talking about harmony, is usually called a suspended ninth) resolving up to the third:

It also appeared in Study 4. This common little lick probably has its roots in country music - it was much used by legendary country pianist Floyd Cramer, for example. Its origins may be in church music, and the decorated plagal suspension that, as we mentioned above, is often used to round off a hymn:

There's a little more left hand movement starting in bar 5, where there's a straightforward left-hand arpeggio. Notice how I'm suggesting that you play the E at the top of the arpeggio with different fingers when it's repeated: the left-hand thumb the first time it's played, and the right hand thumb the second. In the classical tradition different fingers are sometimes used for repeated notes because it allows a cleaner attack on each note. Here it's not really necessary, but I've dropped in the suggested fingering to demonstrate the technique, and repeated it in bars 38-40.

Throughout this section you should focus on being expressive, which - as I mentioned above - means applying a bit of *rubato* and letting the feeling of the music dictate the timing, rather than the underlying beat alone. Since the left hand is straightforward this should be quite easy, but it's worth playing around with different amounts of *rubato*, and using it in different places, just to see what effects you can achieve.

Bars 17-32

With the *tempo giusto* marking we go back to playing strict time. As I said above, when you get confident with this section you can maybe begin to introduce a little *rubato*, but in the first instance you should try to practise this section in strict time.

The section mostly consists of right hand broken chord patterns over a simple left hand, rather like those we saw in Study 3. These will sound best if you play them *legato*, so think carefully about the fingering, even if you choose not to use the fingers I suggest. With the broken chords you need to strike a balance between being even and creating an expressive musical effect: that's going to come down to good control. You might, for example, think about giving a tiny amount of extra emphasis to the highest notes in each bar, or the notes that fall right on the first beat of the bar. Experiment with these bars, maybe practising the right hand by itself at first, and see what different expressive effects you can create.

The left hand is very simple, but there's an interesting effect in bar 27 when the pattern moves from single notes to an octave - you can make quite a lot out of the sudden appearance of the rich, warm, low C# octave in that bar. Resist the urge to be melodramatic in these few bars: keep it restrained and built the power ahead of the more intense section that follows.

Bars 32-49

As we get towards the end of the study, we have more broken chords in the right combined with a left hand that becomes increasingly rhythmic and driving. Take care over the single repeated notes that start on the last beat of bar 38 and end on the first beat of bar 40 with its varied finger pattern (see above). The pattern of rising chords in bars 41-44 needs careful control if you're going to make the most of the *crescendo* effect, the culmination of which should feel like a major release of energy if you get it right.

You'll see, by the way, that part of this section is written in the bass clef for both hands. You'll need to take care that it doesn't end up sounding muddy and confused - a particular risk if you're playing an acoustic piano that's even slightly out of tune. If it doesn't sound quite right on your piano, experiment with moving this section, or at least the right hand, up an octave before returning to the score as written at or around bar 46.

Taking it further

There's quite a lot you can do with this progression, and the study introduces more of the typical sounds and techniques of pop piano, such as the suspended ninth/second lick. Playing around with broken chords could be interesting here, as could taking the progression in a more percussive, upbeat direction, perhaps ending up with effects like those we came across in Study 4.

If you want to make a longer piece out of the study without improvising on it, you'll notice I've added an optional repeated section. If you play the repeat, try varying the expression and dynamics in the repeated section the second time you play it.

Study no. 6

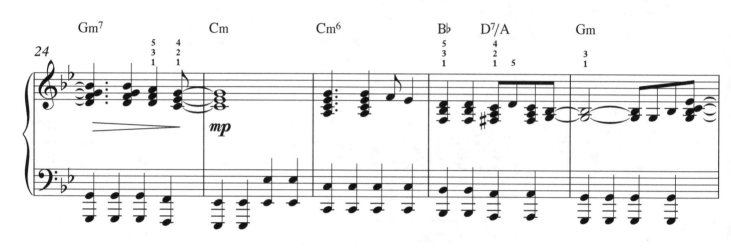

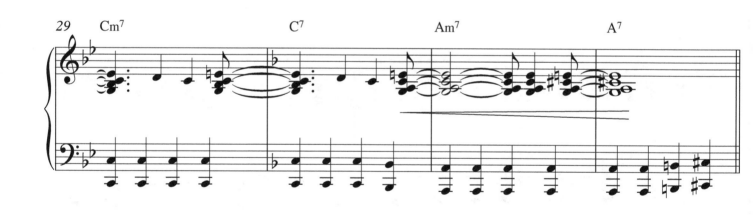

senza ped.

Study no. 6: offbeat metre

This study is a bit different from the others because it has something of a jazzy feel. As I said in the Introduction, pop piano is an incredibly diverse style, and if I included a study that covered every single sound and approach I'd end up with seventy studies rather than seven. However, I thought it was important to include something with this kind of syncopated, off-beat rhythm, because it is, in fact, very common.

In some ways we're back to percussiveness of Study 4, and in terms of the way you physically play, you should definitely think about approaching this study in the same way as that one – with loose, bouncy lower arms (but controlled wrists) and with more of a focus on the overall rhythmic effect than on very fine dynamic control.

The two factors that give the study its particular feel are its off-beat pulse and the 'swung' rhythm of the quavers.

An off-beat pulse is a defining feature of jazz. 'Straight' music – or at least that which has four or two beats per bar – has stressed beats on the odd beat numbers of each bar, which are called the on-beats: *ONE-two-THREE-four*. With an offbeat pulse, the stress is shifted to the even-numbered beats: *one-TWO-three-FOUR*.

The swung quaver rhythm is another feature imported from jazz. It's indicated at the start of the score by this symbol:

$$\sqcap = \overset{\overline{3}}{\sqcap}$$

It means that pairs of quavers that are written as ordinary, equal quavers are actually played as a tripleted crotchet and quaver – a combination that lasts for the same amount of time as two quavers, and in which the first note is twice as long as the second. This doesn't exactly capture the feeling of swing, but it's close (much closer than the dotted quaver-semiquaver pairs that you sometimes see).

The trick with swing is to feel the overall rhythm in the context of the pulse. Once you have the hang of the study you should find that the swing comes fairly naturally – it should just seem like the obvious way to play the quavers against the off-beat pulse.

Harmony

Though there are a lot of chords, the harmony of this study is simple, with few extensions or substitutions. The only real complication is a key change. There's a section in in D minor:

Dm | Dm | Bb | Bb |
Gm7 | Gm7 | C | A7 |
Dm | Dm | Bb | Bb |
Gm7 | Gm7 | C | C ...

44

And a section in Bb major/G minor:

Eb | F | Gm7 | Eb |
Eb | F | Dm7 |Gm 7|
Cm | Cm6 | Bb, D7/A |
Gm | Cm7 | C7 | Am7 | A7...

(Interestingly, although the key signature of this middle section is Bb major/G minor, it's not clear what the key is here. At a push, I'd call it Bb major – even though no Bb chord appears, the overall sound is 'major', F sounds very dominant, and the progression doesn't settle on a Gm chord for very long. Until the bridge passage at the end of the section, if you stop and play a Bb chord, it sounds like the tonic.)

These two progressions fit together in the pattern A-B-A. As I said above, the chords themselves aren't really exotic or spectacular, but they contain some interesting effects (for example, the way D7/A, which doesn't appear naturally in the key of Eb, is used in bar 27 as a passing chord between the chords of Bb and Gm).

Fingering

I've marked some fingering suggestions in the study. As I said above, the percussive effect is what we're after here, so things like *legato* and fine dynamic control don't matter so much. In consequence, the fingers you should use are pretty much the ones you feel comfortable with. In this sort of playing you don't even need to worry too much about total note accuracy: the overall effect is far more important.

However, whatever fingers you decide to use for the chord shapes, you'll inevitably end up doing a lot of jumping around. One of the reasons I've added some suggested fingerings is to show how you might address these jumps.

Expression

As with Study 4, you need to think about your attack: the way your hands and lower arms are working to create the overall effect. You'll probably find that your hands are slightly flattened, with more movement than usual coming from your elbows.

- **Evenness and control.** Although you're playing in a looser, less restrained way than if you were playing (say) a classical piano piece with *legato* sections, you need to take care that things stay under reasonable control and, in particular, don't become erratic, with some chords noticeably louder or 'jabbier' than others – unless that's an effect you want to achieve in particular places, or one that I've specifically suggested (for example, in bars 17-23).

Probably the best way to deal with this is to practise the study in a relatively restrained way first. Learn the notes, then, as your confidence grows, begin to play more aggressively.

• **Dynamics.** The dynamics here are fairly simple: essentially just variations of 'loud' with a few moderately soft bars in the middle section by way of contrast. The trick with loud playing is to avoid charging in as loud as possible right at the start of a piece, except on the rare occasions when doing so is a necessary effect in the song or arrangement you're playing. Give yourself room to get louder still.

• **Pedal.** The sections in D minor (bars 1-15 and bar 41 to the end) and the final part of the middle section (bars 33-40) work best without pedal, so I've marked them *senza pedale*. The lack of pedal will enhance the percussive effect. With pedal, these sections will sound slightly more expansive, but at the risk of creating a booming, ill-defined mess, especially if you're playing an acoustic piano that's even slightly out of tune.

I've marked middle section (bars 16-32) *con ped*. You need the pedal here to stick things together and to give the section a richer sound that contrasts with the minor section. Pedal on chord and bar changes except when a chord change anticipates the start of a new bar (e.g., the last half beat of bar 4, where the Gm7 chord from the next bar comes in early). Also take care that the pedal doesn't fudge the left hand at all, especially when it's playing a non-chord note in preparation for a chord change.

Study no. 6: bar-by-bar breakdown

There's a lot of repetition in this study, so rather than break it down by bar number I've done so by section.

D minor sections (bars 1-16 and 33 to the end)

In terms of actual playing here, there's nothing desperately complicated. The challenge is to stay on tempo and keep the energy levels high without descending into a disorganised mess.

The key to that is the left hand. Even if you're a confident reader, you'll probably find it pays off to play through the left a few times before you try the right. Work on getting those octave stretches punchy and precise, and everything will end up sticking together much better than might otherwise be the case.

The triplet run in the final couple of bars of the study needs to be fast and controlled. How you finger it is up to you: just try to play it as you would a scale, making sure that your thumb isn't thumping down in a way that stands out too much.

Eb middle section and bridge (bars 17-32)

The middle section has a different character from the start and end of the study, and the whole thing will be most successful in musical terms if you can differentiate the two. This section should feel expansive and flowing - you can really let rip here, although you need to make sure you have your playing under control all the time rather than letting it run away with you.

Taking it further

One way you could improvise on this is to make the chord jumps more dramatic - leap around between octaves exploring the effects you can achieve, perhaps experimenting with altering the chords and with suspensions (as I have in, e.g., bar 35).

At all times you should be aiming for control and precision. 'Splashy', imprecise chords can sound quite wild and energetic, but if you choose to play like that it should be a conscious choice, made on the basis of being able to play the notes very cleanly if you choose to.

If you're going to improvise on this study you might find it handy to slow down at first and figure out some possible licks, then speed up as you practise them. Slow practice here should still be regular: try to avoid the kind of poor practice technique that speeds up for the easy bits and slows down for the tough ones.

Study no. 7

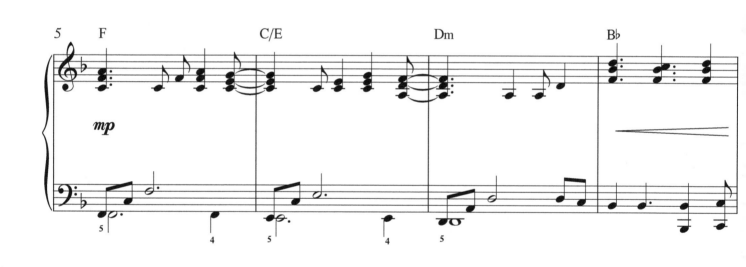

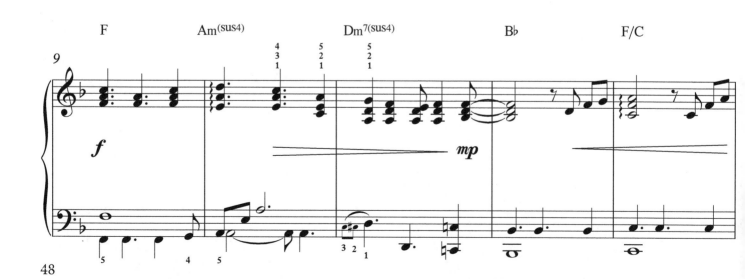

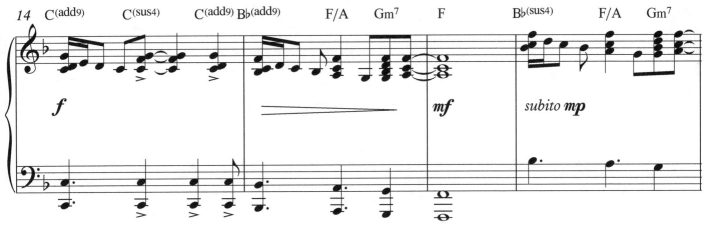

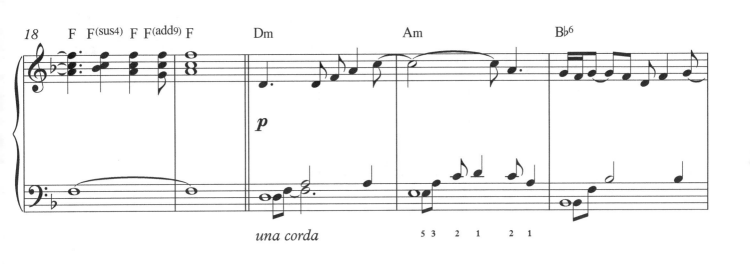

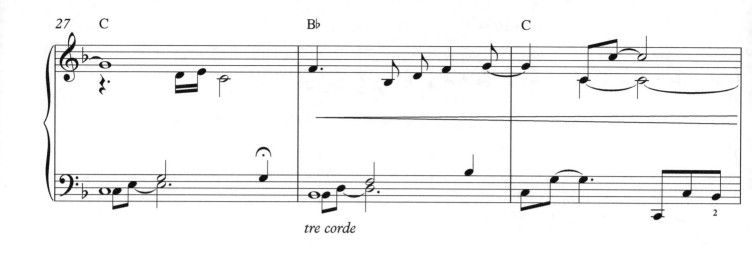

tre corde

D.C. al coda

Coda

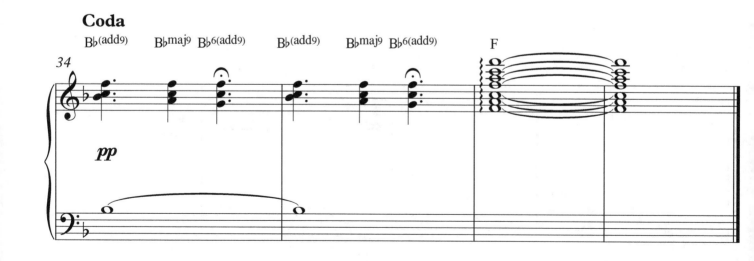

Study no. 7: jumps and sustains

This final study is written in a flowing, rolling style that has deep roots in country music and rhythm and blues. There's a lot of suspensions and anticipation, with harmonies changing and notes and chords coming in half a beat before the start of the bar they 'belong' to.

You'll also notice that many chords are played with sustained arpeggiations and broken chords, occasionally quickly (indicated by an arpeggiation mark, as in the final bar) or over the course of several beats. We've come across this before, for example in Study 5. However, in the earlier studies we generally relied on the pedal to sustain left hand broken chords. Sustaining individual notes by holding them down is harder, but useful, as we'll see.

Harmony

Like Study 6, this study follows an A-B-A pattern. When I wrote the it, the underlying chord progression that I started with was quite simple. Here are the underlying chords of 'A' section:

F | Am7 | Bb | Bb |
F | C/E | Dm | Bb |
F | Am | Dm7 | Bb |
F | C | Bb | F |

And the 'B' section:

Dm | Am | Bb | C |
Dm | Am | Bb| C |
Bb | C | F | Bb |
F | Bb...

Unlike Study 6, the A sections are played identically in this study, as repeats. There's also a three-bar bridge passage after the first A section and a four-bar coda after the second. The bridge section essentially repeats the harmony of the last two bars of the A section, extending the F chord for a further bar. The coda is harmonically distinct from the rest of the study, but uses sounds that have been developed over the course of the piece.

As in previous studies, in the case of harmonic anticipations I've notated the chord change at the start of the new bar rather than on the anticipation (see 'a note on anticipation', p30).

Fingering

In this final study I've notated the fingering only very lightly, indicating the general approach you might take in awkward sections, but leaving the final fingering decisions to you. You'll find that you have to do a fair bit of jumping, and there are some places where you don't have much choice except to 'hop' with your fifth finger in the left hand (e.g. bars 9 and 10) or with your thumb in the right (e.g. bar 4). In the left hand I've tried to vary the rhythms and techniques quite extensively, sometimes sustaining a lower note with the fifth finger while playing repeated notes with the thumb (e.g. bar 12) and sometimes the other way around (e.g. bar 9). There are also some unison octaves (e.g. bar 14) and various different types of broken chord and arpeggio. How you deal with these comes down to what you feel comfortable with, as long as you keep in mind the overall goal of a smooth, flowing sound.

Expression

There are a variety of cross-rhythms in this study, some simple and some complex. The main challenge is to deal with them while keeping up a rolling, fluid forward movement. The study demands a *legato* style – insofar as that's possible, given the need to jump around in places – and doesn't really stray into the sort of percussive playing that we came across in Studies 4 and 6. There's perhaps a slight exception to this around bar 14.

Much of what needs to be said about dynamics, evenness and control we've already covered in earlier studies. However, it's worth saying something about how you might use the sustain pedal in this study. As I mentioned above, creating a sustain effect with held notes allows you to use your discretion much more than if you just use the sustain pedal, and also switch between a rich, full, echoing sound (pedal down) and a precise, tight sound (pedal up) more easily. It can also create more subtle overtone effects than simple use of the sustain pedal allows. Personally, I find that when you use 'finger' sustain in improvisation it also allows greater responsiveness: you're sticking to the keyboard much more closely than if you were releasing notes and letting the sustain pedal carry them. You may find it works differently for you, and that different ways of sustaining work better depending on the piano you happen to be playing.

You'll also notice that I've added an *una corda* direction at the start of the minor section in bar 20. This means 'push down the soft (i.e. left hand) pedal'. You lift it again at the *tre corde* direction at the start of bar 28. The exact effect of this will depend on the type of piano you're playing. The soft pedal on a traditional acoustic grand piano will shift the entire mechanism (including the keys) to the right, so the hammers hit only one string ('*una corda*' in Italian) rather than the three ('*tre corde*') that are allocated to most notes. This softens the overall volume of the instrument and often gives a slightly more muted, gentler tone. On an acoustic upright the soft effect is usually achieved by moving the mechanism closer to the strings, so the hammers can't swing as far. This softens the volume and usually changes the touch and responsiveness of the keys.

On mass market digital pianos, the soft pedal – if there is one – usually just reduces the volume without affecting the tone, which to my mind takes away half of the point of using it. More expensive models often modify the tone to imitate the soft pedal effect on a grand. Anyway, try it on your piano and see what happens. The whole minor section should offer a quieter, restrained contrast to the more expansive sound of the major section, and use of the soft pedal may help you to achieve that.

Study no. 7: bar-by-bar breakdown

Bars 1-7

The study is fairly straightforward to start with. Watch out for the hops with your right hand thumb in bar 4. In bars 5 and 6 there are quite big stretches downwards – thumb to fourth finger over an octave. If your hands are too small for this, or if it's uncomfortable, just jump down with your fifth finger in each case, taking care to smooth over the jump with the sustain pedal.

Bars 8-19

It's in these bars that some of the more challenging cross-rhythms begin to come in. None of them are completely unlike anything we've seen in previous studies, but they are mixed and matched around, sometimes with quite subtle differences between bars. Compare bars 9 and 10 for example, or bars 14 and 15. As usual, if these rhythms seem tricky at first, break them down beat by beat, using the method I described in the notes to Study 4. Remember that, like most pop piano cross rhythms, they should feel and sound very natural when you play them – they just look complicated when you write them down!

The crush notes in bar 11 should be played quickly, so the D comes as near to the beat as possible.

The closest this study comes to a percussive approach is in bar 14, at the top of the *crescendo* with repeated octaves in the bass. I've added accent marks (<) to the notes that you can whack a bit harder. Don't go overboard, though: all you should really be doing is attacking a little more to mark this as the climactic bar of the section.

Bars 20-33

Remember to make this section a contrast to the main section. The only thing you really need to watch out for are the broken chords, which occasionally (e.g. in bars 20, 24 and 28) involve holding three notes, sometimes while playing a fourth at the top with your thumb (no more than two are held at a time in the main section). Make sure you build the *crescendo* in bars 28-29 steadily. In bars 30 and 31, and again in 32 and 33 (an octave higher), you'll see there are a lot of held notes in the right hand, all resolving on to a stripped out Bb(add9) chord. If you play this exactly as written each time, you should get some interesting overtones when you reach the Bb(add9) at the end of each phrase. (By the way, the left hand in bar 31 is supposed to start with a quaver rest, to give a staggered effect. There isn't a missing semibreve.)

Coda

This is quite straightforward. Keep it soft, and experiment with different ways of playing the chords in bars 34 and 35. You can try fingering them *legato* (which is just about possible) or dropping down the Bb, A and G with your thumb, holding things together with the pedal or not, depending on how you like the sound.

The final chord should be arpeggiated quite quickly. You can play all the notes and hold them, but I prefer to tear the chord off quickly by rolling along the notes, more or less lifting each note as the next one is played, and holding the sound of the whole chord with the sustain pedal. There's perhaps a slight difference in sound between the two approaches, but the second one certainly looks more impressive!

Taking it further

There's not much more to add about further improvisation that I haven't covered in previous studies. However, if you do use this study as a basis for improvisation, consider playing around with the structure. Is the best way to extend it simply to repeat the A-B-A structure? Or would something like A-A-B-A work better? Can you redevelop the bridge and coda?

Something else you could try is a modulation to a different key. When pop songs change key it's often a shift of a semitone up (the kind of key change you get, for example, in Whitney Houston's 'I Will Always Love You' or Michael Jackson's 'The Man In The Mirror'). A semitone-up key change can add extra power and drive – which is why songwriters often incorporate one near the end of a song, perhaps after the 2m 30s mark in a 3m 30s song. A good way to handle that in the context of this study might be to play the thing through A-B-A, as it stands, then add an extra A section in the key of F# (or Gb) major. You can achieve the modulation either by simply jumping from the final F chord to a Gb at the start of the new run-through the progression, or modulate using the dominant (or dominant seventh) chord of the new key, like this:

.... F | Db7 —-> Gb etc.

Either method should work fine.

CPSIA information can be obtained
at www.ICGtesting.com
Printed in the USA
LVHW100743090620
657582LV00012B/726